A LAS ORILLAS DEL RÍO VIEJO

A Wesleyan Chapbook

A LAS ORILLAS DEL RÍO VIEJO

a book of poems about
immigrants, trauma,
and perseverance

edited by Katherine Duarte

Wesleyan University Press
Middletown, Connecticut

Wesleyan University Press
Middletown, Connecticut 06459
www.weslpress.org

Wesleyan University Press
Introduction © 2025 Katherine Duarte
All rights reserved
ISBN 978-0-8195-0234-6

Cover Image: *La Mujer Serpiente* ©
By Paul Trujillo

As with all my writing, to my parents

CONTENTS

Introduction

Introduction

The poems in this collection explore the challenges of growing up in the United States with Latino or Caribbean immigrant parents. In particular, these pieces address intergenerational relationships and first-generation trauma, and many touch on cultural disconnection between parents and children. This collection is much-needed in such an uncertain time for immigrants. Each poem here presents a unique narrative about the Latino, Caribbean, or immigrant experience.

I drew inspiration for the book's cover art and title from the Nicaraguan legend of Cihuacōātl, the snake woman. This story of love and grief is a piece of my Nicaraguan culture that is very specifically tied to my mother's life, and to the city that she continues to love and to which she yearns to return. This yearning has caused me a great deal of frustration, especially as I have gotten older and taken on more responsibilities. It is difficult to know that my mother will never settle for a life in the United States, that *home* to her is somewhere across the sea, when home to me will always be *here*, in the only place I have ever known. In a time when immigrant families in the country are being separated, and being used to make examples of, I feel that an intergenerational conversation about home and identity is more important than ever.

--

My mother hated cliffhangers so much that twenty minutes into watching narconovelas on Telemundo she had to switch channels. "They always stop it when it's getting good," she said, lying back on the sofa. "That's how they make their money."

One night when she'd gotten bored of the commercials on Univision, too, she flipped to one of those free channels cable services offered in the early-2000s so they could excuse not including Cartoon Network or HBO with your TV plan. That's how I found out my mother's love for folklore, watching "Lo Que La Gente Cuenta," a Mexican horror anthology where protagonists battle against supernatural forces.

Episodes like *La Llorona* were scary to my seven-year-old mind, but they were nothing compared to the legends of Nicaragua my mother began telling me. Her favorite stories were about *duendes* that slipped into houses at night to find unbaptized children to steal and eat. To this day, she claims she saw one creeping around on my great-uncle's brick ceiling many years ago, the little creature watching, watching, and watching her every move. She also told the story of *La Mocuana,* a legend from Sébaco, the city in northern Nicaragua where she was from. That story, about the betrayal a cacique's daughter faces at the hands of a Spanish conquistador, prompted me to ask her about the founding of Sébaco and where it all—the legends, the people, the history of the stories she told—began.

"La Mujer Serpiente," she answers, and here, you must imagine my mother smiling. It is a very big smile with teeth and sometimes even her molars show if the story is really good. "Cihuacōātl, snake woman, was the wife of a great cacique that ruled what used to be Sébaco at that time. Her

story takes place *en ese tiempo* before the Spanish arrived in Sébaco, when the Sébaco Valley was one. And because she was a cacique's wife, she held more freedoms than the other women in the village. She did not bother with servants to hold her gathering basket. She walked where she pleased. She went and came from the river every day by herself because she simply knew she could. For a time, this did not bother her husband, but as the season turned from dry to wet, the longer she frequented the river, and the more her husband's suspicions grew about what she did alone.

"One day, he decided to follow her and, indeed, Cihuacōātl traveled every day to the river, yet she was not alone any of that time. To the cacique's horror, his wife spent her time in this river with a giant snake wrapped around her body, a creature which that beautiful woman made love to. At that moment a rage so terrible filled the cacique's heart that he killed Cihuacōātl upon her return home. What the cacique did not know, however, was that this giant creature felt a love so deep for Cihuacoatl that when she died it felt her soul leave the Earth, and its anger for her loss was far greater than the cacique's hatred. In its misery, the giant snake slammed itself against the river's waters over and over again, creating a great flood throughout the Valley, separating Sébaco Viejo and Sébaco."

As I look back on my childhood, I think about the constant clashing of values between my mother and me. My rejection of religion, female self-sacrifice, and my disdain for outdated ideas of chastity created a great barrier between us. There are moments when I have felt that becoming my own person has meant abandoning my family's cultural traditions for an immoral, American way of life. Sometimes I do not feel Latina at all. When I was a child, my mother would jokingly threaten to send me back to Costa Rica, where I was born, every time I misbehaved. A great fear consumed me then that I would never see the US again.

We arrived in Miami when I was four, and for the next ten years, I taught myself to reject anything beyond its borders. But at fourteen, I returned to Nicaragua and discovered a deep, unexpected love—for my culture, and especially for my mother's homeland. For the first time, I walked the streets where she had spent most of her life. I laughed with relatives I'd never known, and saw a world so different from the one I took for granted that, when I came back to Miami, I carried with me a longing to understand my mother's past—a life marked by hardship, violence, and pain.

In knowing more about my mother, I seek to carve for myself a path completely different from her own. Is that not selfish? I've been given choices she never had. I've been given freedom. Perhaps this is what we call "guilt." Guilt is the way I try to repay her for all she left behind.

The story of Cihuacōātl involves death and destruction, but at its center is love—a love so deep it changes the land itself. The flood is an act of grief, but also of remembrance and transformation. Immigrants and the children of immigrants carry complex feelings of guilt, pride, and longing, and I am thankful for all of the poets whose work appears in the following pages. I hope that by sharing our stories, we find permission to feel deeply—and to let love, even grief-stricken love, be our guide toward something new.

Please note: the poems by Jennifer Givhan, Scheherazade Samoiloff Ortiz, Jourdelyn "Lyricc" Vargas, and Lorenzo Thomas are rotated vertically in order to preserve the writers' original line and stanza formatting. Similarly, I chose to use a smaller font size for a few of the poems, in order to present the poems without line turnovers.

Katherine Duarte, April 2025

Reynalda's Chair
R. JOSEPH RODRÍGUEZ

Reynalda raises the chair high above her head,
and SLAM! A museum floor of harm and hurt.
(Her shaggy hair like Medusa's in a deep frazzle.)

The people in the seminar are befuddled.
Reynalda rules here and makes it known.
Reynalda decolonizes the rooms and space,
leaving exclamation and question marks.
(Nobody says a word as if silence speaks.)

Reynalda walks away, elegant as a queen.
The seminar comes to an impending end,
and nobody asks what deconstruction is.

Ni de aquí ni de allá
ANDREW GUERRA

I haven't visited Barranquilla in so long
but I can remember the park right across from the house
like it was yesterday.

In Colombia, my accent and my skin tone were mocked.
"Oye Gringo porque hablas raro?" They would say.
"¡No eres Colombiano verdadero!"
But growing up in America
did not make it any easier understanding what home was.

"wetback" and "spic"
They say I'm   "too exotic."
It's almost like I'm neither from here nor from there.
Ni de aquí   ni de allá.

But what exactly does that mean to me?
Where do I go if both sides tell me that I don't belong?
The middle ground is
unclear.

Ni de aquí   ni de allá.

"¡Oye Gringo!"
"wetback" and "spic"

Who am I?

Heart of Darkness and the Horror
JOSÉ B. GONZÁLEZ

Reading Kurtz brings me back
to Chiltiupan. A small field where my
father had taken me to pet a pony.

As we neared the pony's mane,
it lowered and raised its head
in a violent, fast motion.

It bared its teeth, and its eyes
rolled back, scaring my father,
who blocked me from its stomps.

We walked away without talking
about the pony's toe, a cut
of whiteness ready to burst.

A decade later, as I'm reading Kurtz,
his horror, the smell of that toe
begins to seep back into my nose.

My father still won't say a thing
about that pony, the pus, the bleeding
that made him leave us in El Salvador.

Beneath the Sun
CRYSTAL MALDONADO

Before I can
even spell my name,
I've made a habit
of counting my differences.

(One: fat.
Two: not white.
Three: curly hair
Four: parents who never wanted me.)

People ask: "What *are* you?"
But I can't say.
Because well into first grade
I don't know.

Instead, I tell them:
"I am Black.
I am Hawaiian.
I am Jamaican."

(I am wrong.)

Papi hides his Spanish,
Because Mom never liked it.
They say I don't need to say hi abuela
When she calls from "far away."

So, I collect whispers in my pocket
Until I can teach myself that
yo soy boricua,
and my existence is beautiful.

I discover my home stretches
from where I stand
to the Caribbean,
and there's magic in having:

Skin that
glows and
transforms
beneath the sun.

A language
I don't speak,
but that sounds
like music.

Eyes,
dark and damp,
like soil
after a summer rain.

A tongue
that dances
with the taste
of sofrito.

Hair
that breathes
and curves
with the wind.

A body,
like my ancestors,
brown and
soft and strong.

IMPOSTER
QUINN HAYES

my edges are soft unable to break into sisterhood
with expectations for an american black woman to be all around tough

the pressure stemming from the fact we were dealt with worse cards
the grooming of perfectionism to be rewarded and seen, or they call us

unprofessional
underperforming
undeserving

they cringe at my dialect, saying im "trying too hard"
they laugh when i say "nigga"

ostracized when two realities collide

when i straighten my tight ringlets
drop the emphasis on my tone and cut back saying "y'all"
to be invisible for not being relatable

hollow souls collect leftovers, fixating and perfecting pieces of acceptance
which will never be enough to take pride for what my ancestors handed c

"How did you get here?"
MICHELLE HERNANDEZ

Since you asked me after I shared that I'm from
the Bronx, let me tell you how I got here. I got
here the same way you did, by simply applying.
However, even that is hard to know because peo-
ple like you often use their privilege cards to get
what they want. On the other hand, I had good
grades, studied extra hard, went to my teachers
after school, and had countless sleepless nights
trying to be perfect to get myself out of the Bronx.
I earned my way to this campus and left a lot in
New York. Although I wasn't that far, leaving
meant I would see less of my grandparents, par-
ents, and siblings. I learned what it was to care for
someone through them, but I needed to choose
myself for once. So that's another reason why I'm
here; I simply decided to leave home for college. I
got a full ride to my top choice, Fordham Univer-
sity, but I knew I needed a change. I got here by
a 20+ email exchange with the office of Financial
Aid where I was explaining how my parents
financially support others in the Dominican
Republic because they still have family in need
there; all because my financial aid package was
not generous as they asked for about 85% of my
household income. I got here because, during my
junior year of high school, I attended a summer
program this university hosted and became

exposed to dorming life. I connected with the Associate Director of the Office of Admission. She made me want to become a leader because of how she carried herself and followed her heart and passions. I got here by advocating for myself and following my vision. I got accepted to most of my schools all over the country and earned a scholarship based on my grades. But of course, this is all because to people like you who judge people based on where they're from, details from a reality different than yours are gibberish, useless facts. Would you have asked me if I was from the suburbs or looked more like you?

A Manifesto for Dreamers

GINA ATHENA ULYSSE

For Robin D.G. Kelley,
Freedom Dreams: The Black Radical Imagination

When Goya's Saturn picked up his son
and devoured him head first
He wanted to keep him from dreaming

When Goya's Saturn picked up his son
and devoured him head first
He wanted to keep him from dreaming

When Goya's Saturn picked up his son
and devoured him head first
He wanted to keep him from dreaming

A Letter from My Father, Lost at Sea
SUMMER TATE

Mi neva waan tuh be ah fada. Mi waan tuh be ah fishermon.
Spend mi days inna open wata. Smoking mi spliff an
huntin' big fish. Memba wen mi bring *yard* da catfish
an let dem swim inna da bathtub. Yuh madda was mad
bout it. But Im di *Negus* addi house so she know nuh tuh talk.

Mi know dat mi neva did waan tuh be ah fada. Jus ah fishermon
out tuh conquer di sea. For mi skin to turn leather by di salt
an sun. Mi neva mean tuh grow sons an daughters
Jus set da sails of mi ship, an toss mi net tuh haul fish
Tuh feed mi soul. Mi jus waan tuh dash mi line out,
pull in di bounty ah di sea. Set mi eye dem atop di greatness
addi ocean, an explore di unseen *wurl*.

Mi neva waan tuh be ah fada anchored tuh ah fambily
keeping mi pan shore. Ah fishermon charts dem owna course.
Deh live wid di horizon in front dem an shore backa dem.

Mi born pan di island, an mi a island too. Nutten holding mi.
All mi need a sum bait an ah hook.
Mi lure all mi need tuh mi by di rhythm addi sea.
Mi neva need tuh step again
pan ah shore to feel mi ah *yard*.

Mi let di breeze take mi where mi belong far from shore
weathering storms dat try tuh slam mi boat 'gainst jagged
rocks, atop massive waves dat would crush ah lickkle fishermon
tuh flesh an bones. Washin' mi up pan shore broken an beatdown.

Dats why, yuh neva know mi!
Yuh will neva take di scales off mi fish
Yuh will neva welcome mi *yard*.
Yuh will neva mean as much tuh mi as ah fish
caught inna mi net.

Yuh jus' an egg dat hatched di time mi put mi anchor
down pan yuh madda's shore.

Yard – Home
Negus – King

11

Daddy's Lesson
VICTORIA BUITRON

I don't remember the blood.
Nor if the rock felt sanded
by an ancient ocean or if
loose pebbles were left on
my palm. All I remember
is his mom saying that
he had it coming.

If the cut didn't scare
him much, the stitches
would teach him, alright.
My dad loves to tell the story.
He always starts with the catalyst:
my Disney lunchboxes.

I break two in a month.
When he asks why, I confess
it's not me. A boy uses his fists
& kicks until the food leaks
through the cracks. Dad says
if Pablito tries that shit again,
to grab a rock, swing toward his face.

He'll hit me himself if Ariel &
Jasmine come back home broken again.
Today he says that he didn't really think I'd do it.
That of course he'd never hit me,
but he couldn't let his only daughter
grow up to be afraid of boys. Of him?
Yes. But other boys? Never.

Ternura mía
JOSE "CHEPE" SOBALVARRO

Mi triste noche y mi ilusión perdida.
En mi sueño yo la miraba como
una rosa en mi jardín,
bella y hermosa.

¿Ternura mía qué te hiciste de repente?

Sus manos eran como las uvas.
Sus ojos como de cristal.
A mi alma en todo los ámbitos de la vida
nunca pensé en perder mi ilusión.
Nunca pensé que el tiempo
podía cambiar mi vida.
En mi sueño yo la veía,
que se acercaba a mi
con tristezas y más tristezas.

Lo que nunca inmagine,
que noches como estas
iban a ser tan tristes en mi vida.
Y mi tristeza no comparte con mi ilusión.
A nada mi hermosa mía.
Que triste noche pase pensando en ti,
mi ilusión perdida.

Genealogy With Something Sweet for the Voyage
JENNIFER GIVHAN

Mami of the hummingbird feeder Mami hunger/rage & never enough
    sweetwater ever bitterstar ever sugarsap coagulating in Mami's throat—

Mami's mami sold nylons at the department store counter & her mami before
    sewed in the LA garment district & each slapped her hija's face
& some of these/us/our Mamis threatened coathangers. I think of this as I—

    jawless—ride a bus beside a woman carrying pan dulce in a pink box
con Mami of the pig ears Mami of the raspberry-rolled & coconut-shaved Mami

    of the never enough pink for every daughter birthing/burying us—
We eat our fills swilling at the feeder at the hovering dusk
    where no matter how mean/violent/loving we Mamis gather &

slap as masa into cornhusks drenchcoating our icemouths
    our coldest daughtercherried stories fluttering muddown we go—

I Was a Boy
RUBEN QUESADA

As a boy, I was unbearably uncomfortable
about my body and the men my mother dated
gave me erections in the bathroom
as I thought of them under the hiss
of the shower to drown out the catcalls
from boys at school who threatened to kill me

every afternoon. I have tried to avoid
blaming myself for being called a faggot
for most of my life, I could not escape it
but those days have gone like the gospel
of Anita Bryant, who wanted to drown

a faggot rebellion like Stonewall
in the summer of 1969. Once, I was a man
who curated mediocrity like the time
I misspelled peniaphobia to conceal
my fear of having spent my life
penniless, undressing only in the dark.

Retrato de Família
CARLOS DRUMMOND DE ANDRADE

Êste retrato de família
está um tanto empoeirado.
Já não se vê no rosto do pai
quanto dinheiro êle ganhou.

Nas mãos dos tios não se percebem
as viagens que ambos fizeram.
A avó ficou lisa, amarela,
sem memórias da monarquia.

Os meninos, como estão mudados.
O rosto de Pedro é tranqüilo,
usou os melhores sonhos.
E João não é mais mentiroso.

O jardim tornou-se fantástico.
As flôres são placas cinzentas.
E a areia, sob pés extintos,
é um oceano de névoa.

No semicírculo das cadeiras
nota-se certo movimento.
As crianças trocam de lugar,
mas sem barulho: é um retrato.

Vinte anos é um grande tempo.
Modela qualquer imagem.
Se uma figura vai murchando,
outra, sorrindo, se propõe.

Êsses estranhos assentados,
meus parentes? Não acredito.
São visitas se divertindo
numa sala que se abre pouco.

Family Portrait
CARLOS DRUMMOND DE ANDRADE
Translated by Elizabeth Bishop

Yes, this family portrait
is a little dusty.
The father's face doesn't show
how much money he earned.

The uncles' hands don't reveal
the voyages both of them made.
The grandmother's smoothed and yellowed;
she's forgotten the monarchy.

The children, how they've changed.
Peter's face is tranquil,
that wore the best dreams.
And John's no longer a liar.

The garden's become fantastic.
The flowers are gray badges.
And the sand, beneath dead feet,
is an ocean of fog.

In the semicircle of armchairs
a certain movement is noticed.
The children are changing places,
but noiselessly! it's a picture.

Twenty years is a long time.
It can form any image.
If one face starts to wither,
another presents itself, smiling.

All these seated strangers,
my relations? I don't believe it.
They're guests amusing themselves
in a rarely-opened parlor.

Ficaram traços da família
perdidos no jeito dos corpos.
Bastante para sugerir
que um corpo é cheio de surprêsas.

A moldura dêste retrato
em vão prende suas personagens.
Estão ali voluntariamente,
saberiam — se preciso — voar.

Poderiam sutilizar-se
no claro-escuro do salão,
ir morar no fundo dos móveis
ou no bôlso de velhos colêtes.

A casa tem muitas gavetas
e papéis, escadas compridas.
Quem sabe a malícia das coisas,
quando a matéria se aborrece?

O retrato não me responde,
êle me fita e se contempla
nos meus olhos empoeirados.
E no cristal se multiplicam

os parentes mortos e vivos.
Já não distingo os que se foram
dos que restaram. Percebo apenas
a estranha idéia de família

viajando através da carne.

Family features remain
lost in the play of bodies.
But there's enough to suggest
that a body is full of surprises.

The frame of this family portrait
holds its personages in vain.
They're there voluntarily,
they'd know how — if need be — to fly.

They could refine themselves
in the room's chiaroscuro,
live inside the furniture
or the pockets of old waistcoats.

The house has many drawers,
papers, long staircases.
When matter becomes annoyed,
who knows the malice of things?

The portrait does not reply,
it stares; in my dusty eyes
it contemplates itself.
The living and dead relations

multiply in the glass.
I don't distinguish those
that went away from those
that stay. I only perceive
the strange idea of family

travelling through the flesh.

In Colorado My Father Scoured and Stacked Dishes
EDUARDO C. CORRAL

in a Tex-Mex restaurant. His co-workers,
unable to utter his name, renamed him Jalapeño.

If I ask for a goldfish, he spits a glob of phlegm
into a jar of water. The silver letters

on his black belt spell *Sangrón*. Once, borracho,
at dinner, he said: Jesus wasn't a snowman.

Arriba Durango. Arriba Orizaba. Packed
into a car trunk, he was smuggled into the States.

Frijolero. Greaser. In Tucson he branded
cattle. He slept in a stable. The horse blankets

oddly fragrant: wood smoke, lilac. He's an illegal.
I'm an Illegal-American. Once, in a grove

of saguaro, at dusk, I slept next to him. I woke
with his thumb in my mouth. ¿No qué no

tronabas, pistolita? He learned English
by listening to the radio. The first four words

he memorized: In God We Trust. The fifth:
Percolate. Again and again I borrow his clothes.

He calls me Scarecrow. In Oregon he picked apples.
Braeburn. Jonagold. Cameo. Nightly,

to entertain his cuates, around a campfire,
he strummed a guitarra, sang corridos. Arriba

Durango. Arriba Orizaba. Packed into
a car trunk, he was smuggled into the States.

Greaser. Beaner. Once, borracho, at breakfast,
he said: The heart can only be broken

once, like a window. ¡No mames! His favorite
belt buckle: an águila perched on a nopal.

If he laughs out loud, his hands tremble.
Bugs Bunny wants to deport him. César Chávez

wants to deport him. When I walk through
the desert, I wear his shirt. The gaze of the moon

stitches the buttons of his shirt to my skin.
The snake hisses. The snake is torn.

Marlboro Gold 100s
KATHERINE DUARTE

I hate the smell of cigarettes, except
Marlboro,

the same ones my mother stole from my great-uncle when
she was thirteen in Nicaragua.

She's smelled like Marlboro cigarettes her whole life that
she still hides packs in shoe boxes as though she were the
same girl that ran away to Costa Rica, before the existence
of rules, and me, and my brother.

In my grandmother's backyard, my brother and his friend
ripped paper from their notebooks to roll and set on fire.

It was funny to imitate smokers like my mother
who bought cigarettes at the gas station every day
after work. In Calle Ocho, when we took the bus
back home before she learned how to drive,

I found out my mother smelled of grease and ash,
and that her white shirts turned yellow under the arms
because she didn't care that people knew her name
was the only word she understood in

English.

I fucking hate the smell of cigarettes, except
Marlboro, of course,

because they remind me of my mother's hair and clothes.
Marlboro reminds me of her calloused hands and tired feet,
of the silver cap around her tooth she didn't get removed until
after my tenth birthday. When I smell Marlboro cigarettes

I'm brought back to days at a Miami laundromat
when I used to think she would die from cancer,
and my brother and me wouldn't get to steal quarters
to play the old arcade games they kept at the front.

I'll never be a smoker, not even for
Marlboro cigarettes,

but I'll never get tired of the smell of
ash and smoke in my mother's hair, in her clothes,
in her bedsheets, in the trail she leaves behind her
everywhere she walks.

La rubia (The Blonde)

LARA N. DOTSON-RENTA

I loved my grandfather
I was his *rubita*
The little blondie
I had his green eyes
Blond streaks in my hair

He was a beautiful deep shade of brown
Like a spoonful of *helado de tamarindo*

He celebrated *la rubia*
I was light
I was 'white'
And when my children were born they looked
Like me and not him

Who served in a segregated Army unit
In a war somewhere far from the *guanábana* tree
Where he taught me to raise chickens and told me stories
Including one about how he learned what a spic was
On a base somewhere below the 38th parallel

Before the shrapnel and the Purple Heart
The metal shards went with him into the grave

I loved my grandfather
And when he held my daughter in his arms he said
"La rubia"
And he was so proud and enamored
To love a child that did not look like him

Romance Blanco
ALFRED ARTEAGA

There is the man who comes to the door, to
the nine year old girl, "I," does not know him.
No, "No," he puts his foot to the door, kicks,
Her eye, her hand, her nine year leg too waits.
He claims he wants to eat food, "I am nine,
but can talk to a man whose foot breaks here:
the door is mine." This wall, the whole house too.
No one here will give you food. Nor will I.

His boots come from Spain. He has the steel of
his trade at his side. Eyes stare, but no tongue
speaks, "No," or "Si." A nine year old girl stands
still, "I can speak 'No' for man, for him whose
name claims me, 'No' for the one I come from
but can't talk to you man whose foot breaks now.
The voice is mine." This word, the whole word too.
He leaves. Old, dust, smoke-blood, empty dead time.

Medea

SCHEHERAZADE SAMOILOFF ORTIZ

El amor simplemente es, pero ¿por qué es tan difícil aceptarlo?

Tú haces que yo pierda la cabeza.
Quiero que me repitas esas palabras
y las demás que están atrapadas en lo profundo de tu garganta.
Usa la lengua para comunicar. Háblame al estilo de nuestros cuerpos.
Todo lo que necesito se refleja en ti, en esa cara de muñeca,
la que me mira a lo lejos detrás de mis ojos.
Abres la boca y no puedo entender por qué eres una pintura.
Eres bella, una muñeca. Con los labios separados,
tu boca inhalando, esos ojos dulces examinando este cuerpo corrupto.
Me tocas y se convierte en uno puro.
No puedo parar de mirarte la cara.
En una instancia tan íntima, ¿cómo me puedo alejar?
En un momento tan divino, ¿cómo es posible no mirar?
Eres pura esencia. Eres agua bendita.
Me acaloras. ¡Cómo me acaloras!
¡Eres el sol! Eres el sol en las mañanas, en los enredos de la sabana,
y eres el sol hasta en lo oscuro de la noche.
Eres mi sol y me llenas con lo brillante que eres.

¿Te acuerdas?

Ni siquiera fueron días.

No me estés mirando el cuerpo ahora.

¡Aléjate!

Yo te odio, pero yo también me odio a mí misma.

Dime que soy linda,

y nunca pares de decirme.

Nunca será suficiente para mí,

y ya las dos sabemos esto.

Aún no me has perdido. No me vas a perder.

Todo lo que hagas voy a juzgar. Y tú aceptarás.

Aceptarás porque soy una diosa. Soy la única diosa en la que crees.

No es justo, y me fascina.

No voy a dejar que vivas en paz.

No me vas a dejar. No vas a ser la razón de mi vergüenza. No vas a ser una pérdida de mi tiempo.

Te has convertido en mi nieve visual.

I'm there but for the taking
SEAN FREDERICK FORBES

and I'm lucky if we see each other
every other week; a few hours

to connect. Again, you mention how quiet
I am; I'm listening to the timbre

of your voice, the soft giggle
that takes over as soon as you're high.

We've known what it means to be
hungry, drenched from autumnal rain.

We sought survival sex in winter from older
men who took pity, offered vodka room

temperature then bathed us with expensive bars
of soap. I remember the lightness I felt

underneath these men who must have known
I'd pocket some cash—a ten or twenty—

because they always fell asleep so quickly
after. Just yesterday, I found a pair of cufflinks

swiped from a guy on the Upper East Side.
I must have been nineteen. I remember appraising them:

the cabochon sapphires, the tiny single-cut diamonds,
the platinum dog's head. I did well that night.

Contemplated hitching a ride to Jersey to pawn them,
but didn't. Carried them in my pocket for weeks

until I got financial aid and went to classes again.
You're not giggling anymore; it's a hearty laugh, a sneer.

You tell me the root of desperation isn't always the same;
then you pin me to the bed, calloused hands digging

into mine, telling me how easy it'd be to fuck me mercilessly,
that taking what you want when you want it *is* your motto.

Two Ways
ADÉLIA PRADO
Translated by Ellen Watson

From inside geometry
God looks at me and I am terrified.
He makes the incubus descend on me.
I yell for Mama,
I hide behind the door
where Papa hangs his dirty shirt;
they give me sugar water to calm me,
I speak the words of prayers.
But there's another way:
if I sense He's peeking at me,
I think about brands of cigarettes,
I think about a man in a red cape going out
in the middle of the night to worship the Blessed Sacrament,
I think about hand-rolled tobacco, train whistles, a farm woman
with a basket of *pequi* fruit all aroma and yellow.
Before He knows it, there I am in His lap.
I pull on His white beard.
He throws me the ball of the world,
I throw it back.

XI from the *Cantares Mexicanos* (ca. 1550)
EDGAR GARCIA

We all know we'll leave this place.
My question is, what of our race?
When they tell us there's a heaven above
Does it also Indians love?

Are there alcoves of its heart
That still have room for those that depart?
There's been so many who've disappeared
In sickness or darkly financiered.

When they tell us there's a heaven above
Can it spare such infinite love?
What then of its emissaries
Who lash us for our errancies?

We all know our common fate.
My question is, what of their hate?
They hate our kind but profess a love
For us from their ghostly lord above.

Negritude
LORENZO THOMAS

They swim they play the surf for pridefulness
Their slim boards vanity you see them spread over the pages of
                                                          Life hostaged

By photographers who talk like hipsters jewish to their very noses
Infatuate beholden to that scrim of glass and light
The manufactured cataracts of defeated capitalism japanese and german
Eastman Kodak a fine and studied blindness
What will our vacation cost I mean in terms of pride
Mornings when I rise riding the long subway all the way uptown
Half asleep crossing the Columbia campus me glowing in Ferris
                                                          Booth's high glass

I love a slim black boy. I love you
And come to work in my own inferno 300°F. covered with surfboards
Rushing everyday to make the historic effort
But after three days sweat's no catalyst I fear my cop out's from
Exhaustion energy's decomposition by fahrenheitic half-lives not
                                                          arrogance

My father years ago waiting tables in the Tivoli
Won't towel dance the customers to tips runs out screaming Crème
de menthe on rye

Carstairs alamode!
Maybe there never is another job well I'd rather be in alleys & shake
bone dice.

His wife is pregnant in the hospital San Ignaz
Yeah some of that arrogance is me: the break edge of the book, notes
On Function

In placid waves of plate glass or my Nikon's eye, mornings when I rise
The spontaneous book notes what a particular girl says I love you. And
I love you

It is a thing apart from everything the people have.

How to Burn the Village
JOURDELYN "LYRICC" VARGAS

Although death has yet to come into contact with my flesh, life has always felt like a threat to my very existence.

I didn't have my biological parents growing up. See I was met with the foster care system.

A system that was violent: beating me up in every sense. Not quite something a child would expect when parents are the ones meant to love you.

I tried time and time again to be enough.

But enough isn't enough when I take up too much space. I became dependent on my quest to be heard.

Apparently my parents didn't know how to parent me so I began to observe

how I can satisfy their needs.

The Internalized trauma of what I was made to believe. As I would perceive the world with resentment.

I would recognize how I received writing as a form of commitment to liberate myself from the chains of oppression where fear became the intention of manipulation in the home.

Watch your tone. I will kill you if you say anything about what's going on.

It's like his voice is still embedded in my mind. I can't seem to find a place in myself where I feel safe because what if I do speak up, then will I be chased with death?

No, because when I spoke up I gave a voice to my suffering where pain would soon begin to perish.

San Chwa: Chodye Cho
GERARDYE MASSENA

Eskew janm wè le mounn gen problem?
Nou grandi men n'pa janm konnen ki mounn n'ap vini.
Lavi pa dous. Pa met tèt ou sou bèl vi lè de men'w nan chodyè cho.
Lè'w panse pou yon minit ke gen yon bagay kap chanje,
de je'w fèt ap koule de ran dlo.
Eskew janm wè lè mounn gen problem?
Ou poko. Osinon w'pa t'ap swete menm bagay sa pou lavni'w.

Lè lapli tonbe se lè sa ou santiw jwenn lapè.
Lè ate a sèk, tout saw tande se bal kap trible.
Lavi mounn pa fasil se vre
Menm te gen yon lespwa ke pam nan tap chanje.
Ka lè'w panse ou gen lapè,
vreman vre se lè sa lavi'w pral tonbe nan dange.
Eskew janm we lè mounn gen problem?

Lè lot ap tande bèl mizik pou yo ka domi,
mwen menm map tande bal ap grennen.
Wa panse se ka pam ki pi grav.
Tandike lè'm leve poum al lekol nan maten
Mtande se yon lòt pitit ki pran yon kout bal nan domil.
Lè'w kite tèt ou panse se ka'w ki pi mal,
se lè sa'w vinn konnen w'ap viv nan yon lanfè ki pi grav.
Ou met chodye'w cho a midi lè pa gen anyen pou'w bouyi.
Eskew janm wè lè mounn gen problem?

Eskew janm we lè mounn gen problem?
Nou grandi men n'pa janm konnen ki mounn n'ap vini.
Ou met chodyè'w cho a midi lè pa gen anyen pou'w bouyi.
Lè atè a sèk, tout sa'w tande se bal kap trible
Ti lespwa'w genyen an ou santil ap defèt.
Ou grangou, tandike gen yon vwazen'w ki sot mouri
Li pat janm wè lapè.
Eskew janm wè le mounn gen problem?

Hot Pot
GERARDYE MASSENA

Have you ever seen when people have problems?
We all grew up not knowing who we'll become.
Life isn't sweet. Don't set your intentions on it,
not when your hands are scorching in a boiling pot.
Don't think for a minute that something will change
or you will shed rivers of tears.
Have you ever seen when people have problems?
You haven't. Else, you wouldn't have wished the same
for your future.

When the rain falls, you feel at peace.
When the ground is dry, you hear gunshot rounds.
Life isn't easy
but I had hoped that mine would change.
Just when you think you've found peace,
that's when your life slips into danger.
Have you ever seen when people have problems?

While others fall asleep to beautiful music,
I listen for the sounds of bullets raining down.
You'd think my situation was the worst,
yet when I wake up in the morning for school—
Breaking news: a kid was shot in their sleep.
When you let yourself believe your case is the worst,
you realize you're in a hell that's somehow worse.
You put your pot down to cook,
yet noon hits and there's nothing to eat.
Have you ever seen when people have problems?

Have you ever seen when people have problems?
We all grew up without ever knowing who we'll become.
You put your pot down to cook,
yet noon hits and there's nothing to eat.
When the ground is dry, you hear gunshot rounds.
The little hope you built up is now slipping away.
You're starving? Your neighbor just died from it.
All without ever knowing peace.
Have you ever seen when people have problems?

CONTRIBUTORS

R. Joseph Rodríguez is the author of *This Is Our Summons Now: Poems* (2022) and *Youth Scribes: Teaching a Love of Writing* (2025). He lives and teaches in Austin and Fredericksburg, Texas.

Andrew Guerra is a Colombian-American born in Stamford, Connecticut. He is also a recent graduate of the University of Connecticut and an aspiring clinical therapist.

José B. González is the author of *Toys Made of Rock, When Love Was Reels,* and *Tongue Wrapped in Twine* (FlowerSong Press), which will be published in 2026.

Crystal Maldonado is a fat, queer, Puerto Rican author who has written award-winning, inclusive young adult books for readers just like her. Find her at crystalwrote.com

Quinn Hayes was born in a big city and experienced culture shock when she moved to Connecticut's smallest city. This has provided her with inspiration from life's transitions, resulting in the expression of creativity in various forms, with her writing now taking priority.

Michelle Hernandez, a Dominican-American writer from the Bronx, uses her writing to empower underrepresented communities, blending activism and writing to explore identity, culture, and social justice.

Gina Athena Ulysse is a Haitian-American artist-scholar, Professor of Humanities and Founding Director of the RasanblajLab at the UC Santa Cruz.

Summer Tate is a poet and educator with a BA from Bay Path University, an MA in English Education from UConn, and an MFA in Creative Writing from Fairfield University. She is a PhD candidate in English at Howard University.

Victoria Buitron, an Ecuadorian writer who lives in Connecticut, is the 2025 VersoFrontera Prize winner of the poetry collection *Unburying the Bones* (Texas Review Press).

Jose "Chepe" Sobalvarro is a Nicaraguan poet. His upbringing and love for his country's literary influence continue to inspire his work.

Jennifer Givhan is a Chicana + Indigenous poet & novelist who has earned NEA & PEN Emerging Voices Fellowships & published five full-length poetry collections & four novels, including *SALT BONES* (Mulholland/Little, Brown).

Ruben Quesada is a poet, translator, and editor whose collection *Brutal Companion* won the Barrow Street Editors Prize. His work appears in *Best American Poetry, New York Times Magazine,* and Poetry Foundation.

Carlos Drummond de Andrade (1902–1987) was a Brazilian poet and writer. He remains one of the most celebrated Brazilian poets of the 20th century.

Elizabeth Bishop (1911–1979) won the Pulitzer Prize for Poetry for *Poems* (1955), and her book *The Completed Poems* (1969) recieved the National Book Award in 1970.

Eduardo C. Corral is the son of Mexican immigrants. He's the author of *Guillotine* and *Slow Lightning,* which won the Yale Series of Younger Poets Competition. He teaches in the MFA program at Washington University in St. Louis.

Lara Dotson-Renta, PhD is a Puerto Rican writer and educator in Chicagoland. She works between Spanish, English, and French and is interested in how language frames memory and culture.

Alfred Arteaga (1950–2008) is a renowned Chicanx poet and scholar whose work stretches across cultural and linguistic barriers.

Scheherazade "Sheri" Samoiloff Ortiz, an English major at UConn from Puerto Rico, specializes in bilingual poetry and creative nonfiction. She hopes to go into publishing and become a best-selling author.

Sean Frederick Forbes is an Associate Professor-in-Residence in English and the Director of the Creative Writing Program at the University of Connecticut-Storrs. His poems have appeared in *Chagrin River Review, Sargasso, A Journal of Caribbean Literature, Language,* and *Culture, Crab Orchard Review,* and other publications. *Providencia,* his first book of poetry, was published in 2013.

Adélia Prado was born and has lived all her life in Divinópolis, Minas Gerais, Brazil. She began publishing her poetry when she was forty, and since then she has published eight books of poems and poetic prose.

Ellen Watson is a prolific translator and has translated several books from Brazilian Portuguese into English.

Edgar Garcia is a poet and scholar of the hemispheric cultures of the Americas. His most recent book is *Emergency: Reading the Popol Vuh in a Time of Crisis.*

Lorenzo Thomas (1944-2005) was a critic and poet who published many volumes of scholarship as well as numerous essays, including several histories of the Umbra group.

Jourdelyn "Lyricc" Vargas is the author of *Mi Gente, Let's Get Personal.* She uses poetry to spark connections, amplify voices, and create a space rooted in understanding and authenticity.

Gerardye Massena is a graduate student earning a master's degree in biomedical science. She immigrated from Haiti as a teenager and now shares her story as a first-generation student and child of immigrants.

Katherine Duarte is a graduate of the University of Connecticut. She is a fan of all things fantasy and updates her Goodreads account more than a writer changes words. In her literature classes she'd say that her favorite book is *The Robber Bride* (because she loves talking about moms as much as Tony loves talking about war), when in truth it's probably still *Heartless* by Marissa Meyer or Holly Black's next big release. Her work has been published in *New Square*, *Inverted Syntax*, and the essay collections *Fast Fallen Women* and *Fast Famous Women* by author and professor Gina Barreca.

(🌺)

Poems in this chapbook originally appeared in the following books:

Ulysse, Gina Athena. "A Manifesto for Dreamers." *Because When God Is Too Busy*, Wesleyan University Press, 2017.

Givhan, Jennifer. "Genealogy With Something Sweet for the Voyage." *Belly to the Brutal*, Wesleyan University Press, 2022.

Andrade, Carlos Drummond de. "Retrato de Família." *An Anthology of Twentieth-Century Brazilian Poetry*, edited by Elizabeth Bishop and Emanuel Brasil, Wesleyan University Press, 1997.

Arteaga, Alfred. "Romance Blanco." *Xicancuicatl: Collected Poems*, edited by David Lloyd, Wesleyan University Press, 2020.

Prado, Adélia. "Two Ways." *The Alphabet in the Park*, edited by Ellen Watson, Wesleyan University Press, 1990.

Garcia, Edgar. "XI from the Cantares Mexicanos (ca. 1550)." *Cantares*, Wesleyan University Press, Forthcoming 2026.

Thomas, Lorenzo. "Negritude." *The Collected Poems of Lorenzo Thomas,* edited by Aldon Lynn Nielsen and Laura Vrana, Wesleyan University Press, 2019.

All other poems in this collection are new and previously unpublished, and appear here by permission of the authors.

"Reynalda's Chair" by R. Joseph Rodríguez from *Entre Magazine of the Arts, vol. 1, no. 1.* Copyright © 2024 R. Joseph Rodríguez. Used by permission of author.

"Daddy's Lesson" by Victoria Buitron from *Mythic Picnic.* Copyright © 2022 Victoria Buitron. Used by permission of author.

"I Was a Boy" by Ruben Quesada from *The Seneca Review.* Copyright © 2024 Ruben Quesada. Used by permission of author.

"In Colorado My Father Scoured and Stacked Dishes" by Eduardo C. Corral from *Poetry.* Copyright © 2012 Eduardo C. Corral. Used by permission of author.

Special Thanks to Suzanna Tamminen, Gina Barreca, Sean F. Forbes, Paul Trujillo, Emily R. Schwab, and The Helen Gurley Brown Foundation.

Wesleyan Chapbooks

Entanglements by Rae Armantrout

Notice by Rae Armantrout

The Poetry Witch Little Book of Spells by Annie Finch

I Will Teach You About Murder: 29 Love Poems, Edited by Shea Fitzpatrick, Sallie Fullerton and Torii Johnson

I Said That Love Heals from Inside: Love Poems of Yusef Komunyakaa by Yusef Komunyakaa, Edited by Oliver Egger

I Ask My Mother to Sing by Li-Young Lee, Edited by Oliver Egger

Deaths of the Poets by Kit Reed, Illustrated by Joseph W. Reed

Dog Truths by Kit Reed, Illustrated by Joseph W. Reed

Thirty Polite Things to Say by Kit Reed, Illustrated by Joseph W. Reed

www.ingramcontent.com/pod-product-compliance
Lightning Source LLC
Chambersburg PA
CBHW071734020426
42331CB00008B/2019